THE ANCIENT NEAR EAST

by Malcolm Yapp

AF875004

Greenhaven Press, Inc.
577 SHOREVIEW PARK ROAD
ST. PAUL, MN 55112

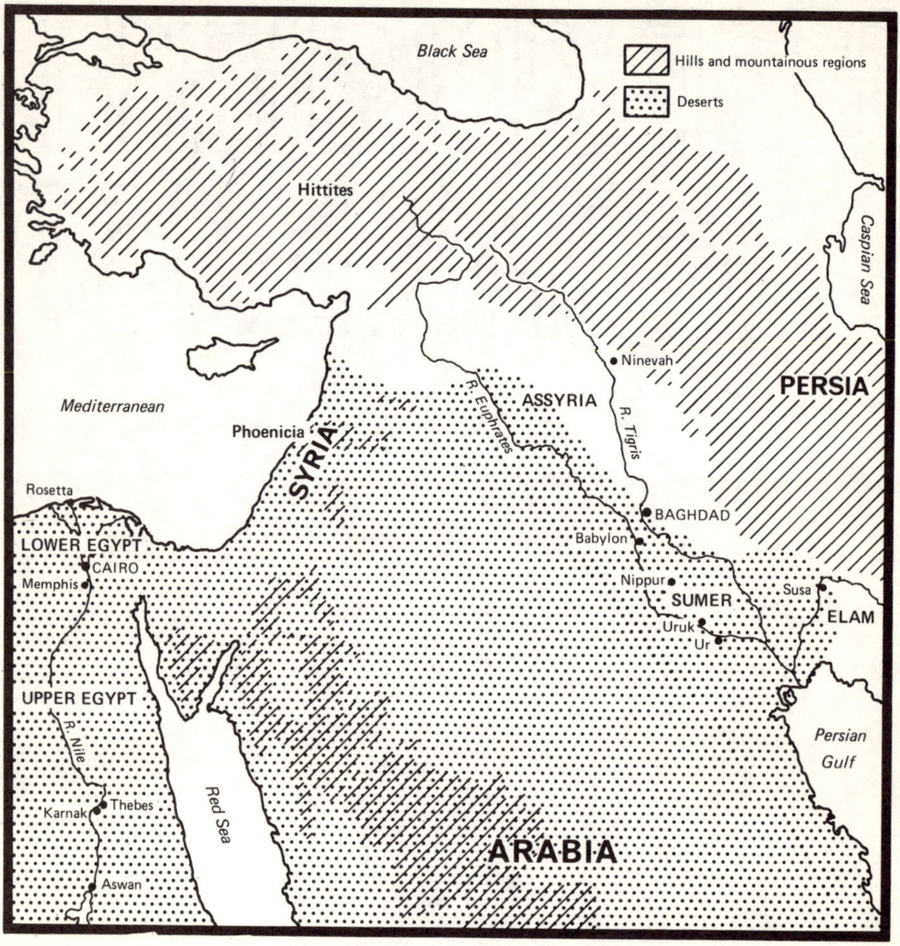

The Ancient Near East

'HISTORY BEGINS AT SUMER'

It is said that history begins about 3000 B.C. at Sumer, a small area in the south of the modern state of Iraq. Why? The answer is simple: the people of Sumer invented writing.

History begins with the invention of writing. By studying bones, tools, pots, etc., archeologists can tell us a lot about peoples who could not write. But such peoples could not tell us about themselves in their own words. Without written evidence we can never know what people thought, or wanted, or even their names. But we are able to know people who could write, and who left records that we can read, in quite a different way. We call that way history.

CITIES AND CIVILIZATION

Something else quite new happened at Sumer: men built and lived in cities. By our standards they were only small towns. But

A round boat on the Tigris, circa 700 BC

the move into towns meant a different way of life.

In another booklet *(Man and Food)** you can read about the neolithic revolution, when men who had previously lived by hunting and gathering wild plants began to keep their own domestic animals and to grow their own food. It was this change which made it possible for men to live in cities. When they grew their own food they could be more sure that it would be there and could also have more food available. So some members of the family were able to stop food gathering – they ate food provided by others – and were able to concentrate on other things. People began to specialize in the things they could do best.

Cities depend on specialization. They depend on food from outside to support the workers in the city. The food produced in the countryside had to be exchanged for goods made in the city. To organize this exchange required a new type of government and the beginnings of the state.

Writing, cities and government: the three together form the basis of what we call civilization. They first appeared in the ancient Near East.

THE ANCIENT NEAR EAST

The Near East stretches from Egypt to Persia. It may seem a strange place for civilization to begin, for it has few natural resources and in the summer is very hot and unpleasant. Some historians have said that it was partly because it was so difficult to live in the Near East that civilization first developed there; the difficulties forced men to find new ways to live, while in places where life was easy they could go on gathering the food around them.

Geographically the Near East is divided into two areas; the mountains of the north and the

*Titles in brackets refer to other booklets in the Program

SUMERIAN CITY STATES	*3000-2400 BC*
FIRST SEMITIC EMPIRE	*2400-2200 BC*
SUMERIAN REVIVAL (Third Dynasty of Ur)	*2100-2000 BC*
SECOND SEMITIC EMPIRE (Old Babylonia)	*1900-1600 BC*
ASSYRIAN EMPIRES	*1400-600 BC*
539 BC Babylon captured by the Persians	

Time chart of Ancient Iraq

deserts of the south. In two areas the desert has been made fertile by large rivers. These fertile areas are in Iraq and Egypt. Through Iraq flow the Tigris and the Euphrates on their way southwards from the mountains to the Persian Gulf. Through Egypt flows the Nile on its way northwards from the mountains and lakes of east and central Africa to the Mediterranean. These rivers bring with them fertile soil, in which plants grow easily, and the water to make them grow.

A date plantation in Iraq

ANCIENT IRAQ

More than five thousand years ago some neolithic farmers began to move from the mountain valleys to the plain of Iraq. The change was very great. In the mountains rain made crops grow. But in nearly all the plains there was not enough rain. To grow food the farmers had to learn how to use the rivers to obtain water: to dig ditches to lead the river water to their fields when they were dry and to lead the water away in the spring and early summer when the rivers flooded. It was hard work and if the floods were too great or too small the results were disastrous and people starved. But if they could control the river the rewards were great because the soil was so fertile that one kilo of barley seed would give back 89 kilos at harvest time. Also, the rivers held fish to eat and in the delta of the south dates grew in plenty. With proper organization it was possible to grow enough food to make civilization work. (D1, 2, 3)*

SUMER

The first civilization of Iraq was that of Sumer. The Sumerians left their records on clay tablets. When the clay was wet they drew on them with reeds and then baked the clay so that the writing became permanent. They did not leave these records for us, of course; they kept records because they needed them in their daily lives to record bargains, legal decisions, etc. Some are school essays. From these tablets we can construct a picture of how the Sumerians lived. They lived in city states. At the centre of each city was a temple, a collection of buildings with the people who worked in them. The main temple building was called a *ziggurat*. This was made up of several brick platforms, one on top of another, rising to a height of thirty metres or more. The temple was served by priests and scribes and ran schools to train writers. There were also streets in which workers and craftsmen lived. Later there was a citadel for defence and government offices. We know about all these from the records which were left by the scribes who were connected with the temples.

EVIDENCE

The fact that it was the priests or scribes who kept most of the early records leads to an important point which we have to remember, not only when we are studying the ancient Near East, but when we are studying any history. When you see a document you must ask who wrote it and why he wrote it. The documents from Sumer were written mostly by priests for their own purposes. Reading them we may think that Sumer was run by priests. Some historians think this was the case and that the Sumerian cities and their lands belonged to gods and were run on their behalf by priests. But we cannot be certain that this is true. There may well have been other people who owned lands but who could not write and so we don't know about them.

*The reference (D) indicates the numbered documents at the end of this book.

TABLET OF MORAL PRECEPTS
INCLUDING WARNINGS TO
KINGS CONCERNING THE EVILS
WHICH FOLLOW
MISGOVERNMENT AND INJUSTICE.

Opposite page: A Sumerian clay tablet giving rules for kings

METALS AND TRADE

The Sumerian craftsmen worked in wood and metals. The main metals used to make tools and weapons were first copper and then (by mixing the copper with tin) bronze. But Sumer had neither trees, nor copper, nor tin. All had to be imported from the mountains of the north. To pay for them the Sumerians had to develop their own industries – mainly textiles – and export their products in exchange. Thus, the development of specialization in crafts made trade necessary. The river valley made trade easier because boats could be used. (D4) A class of merchants grew up to carry on this trade. The merchants not only carried goods but they also carried ideas. The people of Iraq began to develop the first systems of weights and measures, and then, because it was easy to express weights in terms of the weight of a piece of silver or gold, they began to develop a system of money.

ASSYRIA AND BABYLONIA

We have looked at some connexions between the people of the river valley and those of the mountains. A third group of people who were very important in the history of ancient Iraq were the people of the great deserts which stretch from Arabia right up between the fertile areas of Syria and Iraq. These were nomads who lived by tending their flocks of sheep and goats, in the oases or along the river banks. There was constant friction between them and the people who lived by growing food.

The nomads were, however, powerful and warlike and they encroached on the cities of Sumer and eventually took over control of the whole area. The new rulers

Model reconstruction of the ziggurat at Ur

Assyrian statue found at Nimrud

spoke a language (Akkadian) which was different from that of the Sumerians and belonged to a family of languages called Semitic – the same as Hebrew and Arabic. But the Akkadians adopted much of the Sumerian way of life including their way of writing. We actually have dictionaries which they compiled to help them in their writing.

Many Akkadian empires rose and fell. The Akkadians spread outside Sumer to the north and there they built their capital cities including Babylon and Nineveh (the capital of Assyria). (D5, 6, 7) From the chronicles and inscriptions which the great Babylonian and Assyrian rulers left, as well as from the writings of the Jews and the Greeks, we know a lot about these empires, but the details of their great battles do not matter to us here. What concerns us is what their empires were like.

GOVERNMENT

We are not sure how the first cities were ruled. They may have been ruled by priests or they may have been ruled by agreement between the more important citizens. In the course of time a struggle for power took place at the end of which men called *lugals,* which means big wigs, came out on top. Eventually the big wigs became kings and with the arrival of the Akkadians the authority of the kings rapidly grew as they developed strong armies and large bureaucracies (offices and officials). The kings ran the state and in their inscriptions and annals they boasted about how powerful they were and what great deeds they had done.

ARMIES

The first armies were small and probably consisted only of the men of each city who were fit and able to fight. They fought on foot with axes and spears. Such armies were not much use to the later kings whose minds were turned to conquests in the north, in Syria and even in Egypt. (D8) For their great campaigns they needed professional armies with foreign mercenaries and skilled officers. Armies became much larger and better equipped. One of the most important changes took place about 1500 B.C. when the chariot was introduced. Before that time there were only heavy carts with solid wheels. They could be pulled only by oxen and were far too slow to be of any use in battle. The invention of the spoked wheel made carts much lighter so that they could be pulled rapidly by horses. As rapidly manoeuvrable fighting platforms they were devastating on the battlefield. Later (after about 1000 B.C.) men began to fight from the backs of horses and cavalry gradually replaced chariots. Another formidable weapon was the compound bow, a curved bow made of pieces of wood and horn carefully glued together. The compound bow could shoot arrows over long distances and with such force as to penetrate armour. Finally the basic weapons of swords, spears and axes had also changed. In the northern mountains of Anatolia a people called the Hittites had

Time Chart of Ancient Egypt

First period	
Dynasties 1-2	*3100-2700 BC*
Old Kingdom	
Dynasties 3-8	*2700-2200 BC*
First period of troubles	
Dynasties 9-11	*2200-2000 BC*
Middle Kingdom	
Dynasty 12	*2000-1780 BC*
Second period of troubles	
Dynasties 13-17	*1780-1550 BC*
New Kingdom	
Dynasties 18-20	*1550-1075 BC*
The Decline	
Dynasties 21-31	*1075-332 BC*
Greek Period	*332-20 BC*
Roman Period	*30 BC- AD 395*
Byzantine period	*AD 395-640*

Opposite page:
Detail of Assyrian soldiers

discovered how to work a new, stronger metal: iron. Although they kept the secret for many years the knowledge gradually leaked out and spread all through the Near East after about 1200 B.C. Iron had many peaceful uses but one of its principal uses was for war because it was so much harder than bronze.

The great Assyrian and Babylonian armies of around 600 B.C. were very formidable armies with their trained officers, skilled soldiers, their chariots, cavalry, infantry and their new weapons. The Bible tells us a great deal about their deeds. Such armies made it possible to build new empires covering great areas. They also made the creation of such empires necessary because the armies always needed more money to keep them happy and money had to be raised either by taxes or by loot from new conquests. It was an age of violence organized on a new scale.

LAW

To live together in the city states and the empires of ancient Iraq, people needed laws. From Sumeria comes the first code, or collection of laws, and this was enlarged by later rulers. The largest and best known code of laws was that of the Babylonian Emperor Hammurabi (c. 1792-1750 B.C.). Most of his laws were civil laws, that is laws dealing with the family, land rights and trade. Some were laws about crime. The laws tell us much about the society

View of the Nile

of the time. People were not equal. Women came off badly, especially in later times. Nobles had rights that poor men did not have. (D9, 10, 11) Society was developing the structure and shape of civilization.

EDUCATION

The main purpose of education was to train scribes: men who could read and write and so serve the temple, the palace, the law courts and trade. Only a very few people ever learned to read and write. A few, however, went on to other studies: mathematics for keeping accounts; astronomy in order to be able to prophesy the future, for men thought that the explanation for many events on earth lay in the skies; and medicine in order to treat the sick. (D12)

ANCIENT EGYPT

The valley of the Nile resembles that of the Tigris-Euphrates in many ways but there are some important differences. The rivers of Iraq are wild rivers with great floods that spread all over the plain and obliterated whole cities. They are difficult to control. The Egyptian Nile is more peaceful. Each year it floods from July to October. The water was led off into the fields through channels and later allowed to run back into the river. Seed was planted in the fertile mud that was left. When the river was low, water was lifted by hand and later by the *shaduf*, a bucket fixed on the end of a length of wood, which was balanced and pivoted on a fulcrum. By using this lever a man could lift 4500 litres of water a day. The wheat and barley were harvested by May before the next floods. In this way much of the work was done in the cooler months of the year, unlike Iraq where the seed had to be planted and tended through summer. The sides of the Nile Valley were higher than the river and it was easy for people to live there and escape drowning in the floods. So although there were periods of famine in Egypt they were not so bad as those in Iraq. (D13, 14)

The Egyptians had yet another advantage. All along the Nile Valley was stone which could be used for building, and which lasted much better than the baked clay with which the Iraqis had to work.

Life was probably easier in Egypt and it may have been partly because of this that things moved more slowly in Egypt than in Iraq. Although Egyptians were obliged to trade with other countries, especially to obtain wood, they did not develop such large-scale trade as the people of Iraq and never had a class of merchants. Nor did they adopt new ideas so quickly. Most of the major changes came into Egypt from outside. The Egyptians were slow to change from copper to bronze, and slower still to change to iron. Their system of law was not so developed as that of Iraq; they do not seem to have had a code of laws. (D15) Their education was similar to that of Iraq but they do not seem to have advanced so far in the study of mathematics and astronomy. Clever as it was their system of writing did not develop so quickly as that of Iraq. Both systems

A shaduf

Series of shadufs used to raise water to a higher level

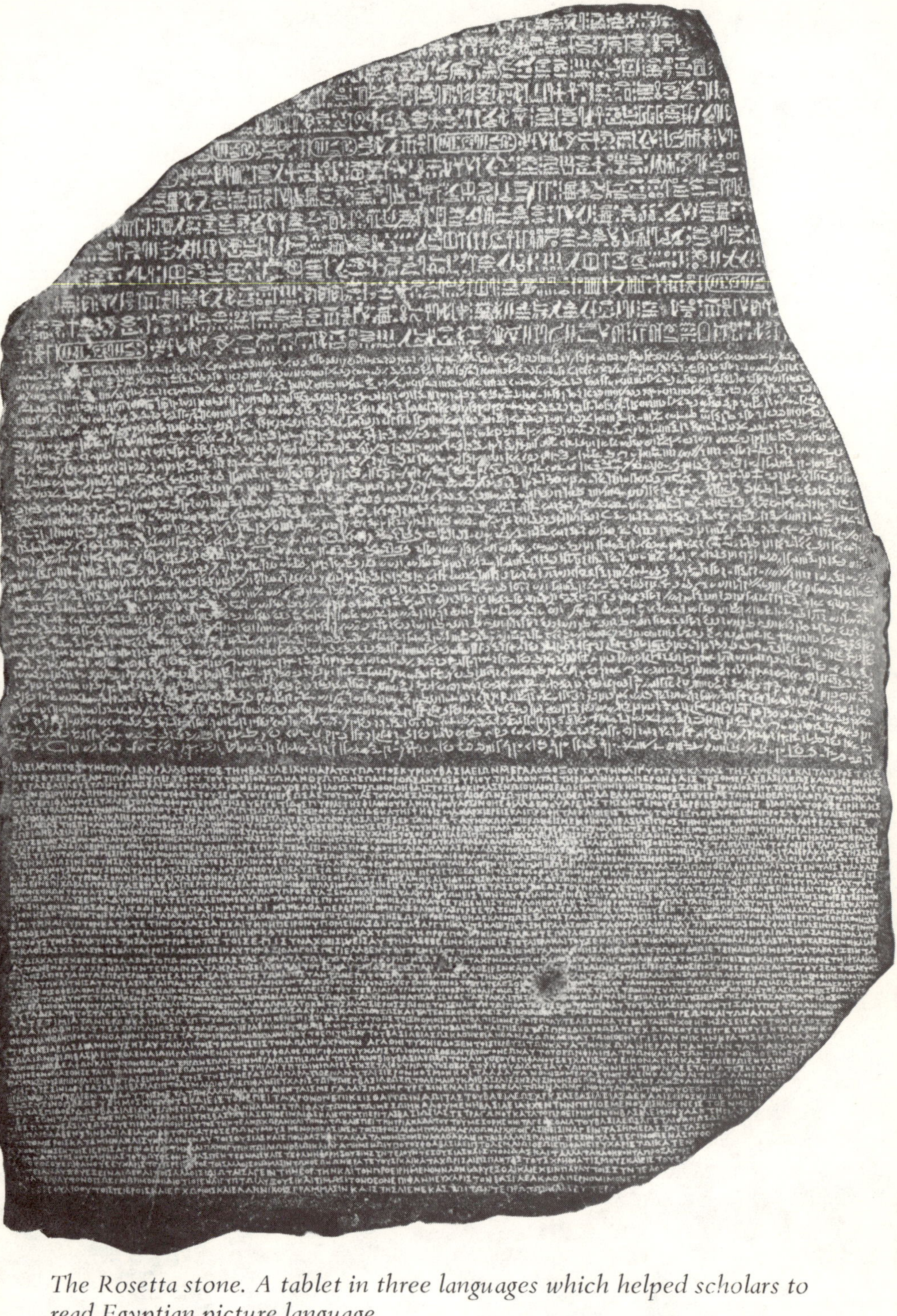

The Rosetta stone. A tablet in three languages which helped scholars to read Egyptian picture language

The oldest pyramid; the Step pyramid at Sakkara

began with drawing pictures of things. But whereas the people of Iraq soon changed to a phonetic alphabet, that is, one in which the signs or letters represent sounds and not pictures, the Egyptians only did this to a limited extent. The result was that the Egyptian system remained more awkward and made it more difficult to express certain abstract ideas. (D16, 17)

BUILDING AND CRAFTS

The Egyptians excelled in building and crafts. Working in gold, other metals and wood they made the finest articles. Working in stone they left some of the mightiest buildings in the world. Near the ancient capital of Memphis, near Cairo, are the great tombs called the pyramids which were built c. 2700 B.C. Farther south at the later capital of Thebes, is a great city of the dead. Nearby, at Karnak, are mighty temples.

To construct these great buildings of stone the ancient Egyptians did not have advanced tools and techniques. They built with patience, hard work and the application of human labour on a scale never seen before. To build the pyramids great slabs of stone had to be split off the hills with wooden wedges, trimmed with stone axes, floated across the Nile on great rafts and hauled by men up enormous inclined planes of sand to be set into position. The largest pyramid, the Great Pyramid, contains 2 300 000 blocks of limestone of an average weight of 2.8 tonnes each. It was

The Sphinx and the Great Pyramid at Giza

Temples at Karnak

The Valley of the Dead at Thebes

built in 23 years, which means that on average 300 stones were cut, dressed and put into position every day.

GOVERNMENT

The work involved in such buildings suggests that the Egyptians had developed ways of organizing people for peaceful purposes to a greater extent than other societies of the time. In other words, the government was stronger. What sort of government did the ancient Egyptians have?

At the head of the government was the king (later called pharaoh). In theory he was much greater than the rulers of Iraq, because he was believed to be a god and everything was supposed to belong to him. In practice of course he could not do everything and the work was done by a large bureaucracy of priests and officials headed by a chief minister. The officials administered the law, collected taxes, arranged for defence and organized building.

Much of our knowledge of ancient Egypt comes from tombs, in which are found many inscriptions and rolls of papyrus (paper made from reeds). (D18) If you are looking at life from the

Rameses II, an Egyptian king of the New Kingdom

point of view of death and the burial of the dead, you may get an odd view of it. This may account for some of the apparent strangeness of ancient Egypt.

The Egyptians spent a lot of time and money looking after the dead. The tombs were of great size and splendour and were filled with the most magnificent treasures. As it happened most of the tombs were robbed, probably soon after the burials, but one tomb, that of Tutankhamen, has been discovered intact. (D19, 20) It contained more than 1300 kgs of gold. Strangely enough, although their treasures disappeared, the kings did not, because they were embalmed or mummified (that is, the bodies were specially treated to preserve them) and the mummies of many of the kings were found. They have now been unwrapped and lie in glass cases in the Cairo Museum of Egyptian Antiquities. There you can see the men who had such power, so long ago. (D21)

The kings in the museum were the rulers of Egypt during its greatest period, that is during the New Kingdom (1550–1075 B.C.). That was a time of Egyptian revival, following a period when they had been ruled by kings from Asia, the Hyksos. (D22, 23) The Egyptians learned a lot from the Hyksos and the kings of the New Kingdom adopted the new military techniques (including the chariot), organized large professional armies, and marched into Syria where they fought the Hittites. But the New Kingdom was an exceptional period. Most Egyptian kings preferred to stay at home and guard their frontiers. There were also periods when Egypt had weak rulers. Even under the strong rulers the authority of the king was mainly in Upper Egypt, the area south of Cairo. In the north, in the Delta of Lower Egypt, it was much more difficult

Tutankhamen's state chariot

for the king to keep control. In the provinces there were always independent local governors and nobles; and in the deserts the nomads were difficult to control. Although we can say that the organization points to a strong government we must not think that it compared with modern governments.

THE ANCIENT NEAR EAST IN WORLD HISTORY

There is much that we do not know about the ancient Near East. Because of this we should be careful not to be too confident about what the Egyptians and Iraqis thought and did. But what we do know is that the people of this area laid the foundations of civilization. In politics they invented governments, kings, bureaucracies, professional armies and police forces. In social life they built the first cities; developed the first great religious systems and organizations; made the first legal systems; began the first schools; and explored knowledge. In economics they

Models of Egyptian soldiers, circa 1900 BC

developed the first regular trade and money. Above all they began to write and to leave records.

These ancient peoples did these things because they took the great decision to specialize and organize – the choices made possible by the neolithic revolution. *(The Neolithic Revolution)* The change took place in the great river valleys because these areas had the right conditions to produce a large food surplus and to organize people and their activities over a large area. It is also in the valleys of the Yellow River in China, the Ganges in India, and the Indus in Pakistan that we see other ancient civilizations.

DOCUMENT 1

IRRIGATION IN IRAQ 1 – NORTHERN IRAQ *HERODOTUS – Greek historian who lived during the fifth century B.C.*

Little rain falls in Assyria, enough, however, to make the corn begin to sprout, after which the plant is nourished and the ears formed by means of irrigation from the river. For the river does not, as in Egypt, overflow the corn-lands of its own accord, but is spread over them by the hand, or by the help of engines. The whole of Babylonia is, like Egypt, intersected with canals. Of all the countries that we know there is none which is so fruitful in grain. It makes no pretension indeed of growing the fig, the olive, the vine, or any other tree of the kind; but in grain it is so fruitful as to yield commonly two hundred fold, and when the production is the greatest, even three hundred fold.

DOCUMENT 2

IRRIGATION IN IRAQ 2 *STRABO – The Greek author of the first general book on geography (born c. 63 B.C.)*

The Euphrates rises to flood at the beginning of summer, rising first in the spring when the snows in Armenia melt, so that of necessity it forms lakes, and floods the ploughed lands unless the surface water is taken off by means of canals. Much labour is required to maintain the canals because the soil is so deep and soft and yielding that it is easily swept out by the streams and the plains are laid bare, and the canals are easily filled and choked by mud, so that the water overflows again, emptying into the plain near the sea and forming lakes, marshes and reed beds.

It is impossible perhaps to prevent overflows of this kind, but it is the job of good rulers to help as much as possible by building dams, and keeping the canals free from mud. Now the clearing of mud is easy, but to build dams requires much work because the earth is soft and easily collapses under the weight of the mud which is washed on to it.

Also it is necessary to work fast in order to close the canals quickly so as to stop all the water emptying out of them. For when they dry up in summer they dry up the river too and when the river is low it cannot fill the canals at the time when water is most needed in summer when the country is fiery hot.

DOCUMENT 3

INSTRUCTIONS TO A SUMERIAN FARMER *From a Sumerian clay tablet, about 2000 B.C.*

When you are about to cultivate your field, take care to open the irrigation works so that the water does not rise too high in it. When you have emptied it of water, watch the field's wet ground that it stays even; let no wandering ox trample it. Chase the prowlers and have it treated as settled land. Clear it with ten narrow axes weighing no more than two thirds of a pound each. Its stubble should be torn up by hand and tied in bundles; its narrow holes should be dragged and the field fenced. During the hot weather divide the field into parts. Let your tools hum with activity.

DOCUMENT 4

BOATS ON THE EUPHRATES *HERODOTUS*

But the greatest wonder of all that I saw in the land, after the city itself, I will now proceed to mention. The boats which come down the river to Babylon are circular, and made of skins. The frames, which are of willow, are cut in the country of the Armenians above Assyria, and on these, which serve for hulls, a covering of skins is stretched outside, and thus the boats are made, without either stem or stern, quite round like a shield. They are then entirely filled with straw and their cargo is put on board after which they are suffered to float down the stream. Their chief freight is wine, stored in casks made of the wood of the palm tree. They are managed by two men who stand upright in them, each plying an oar, one pulling and the other pushing. The boats are of various sizes, some larger some smaller; the biggest reach as high as 150 tons burthen. Each vessel has a live ass on board; those of larger size have more than one. When they reach Babylon, the cargo is landed and offered for sale; after which the men break up their boats, sell the straw and the frames, and loading their asses with the skins set off on their way back to Armenia. The current is too strong to allow a boat to return up-stream, for which reason they make their boats of skins rather than wood. On their return to Armenia they build fresh boats for the next voyage.

DOCUMENT 5

THE ASSYRIAN KING SENNACHERIB DESTROYS BABYLON

An inscription by Sennacherib, 703 B.C.

The city and its houses, from its foundation to its top, I destroyed, I devastated, I burned with fire. The wall and the outer wall, temples and gods, temple towers of brick and earth, as many as there were, I razed and dumped them in the Arakhtu canal. Through the midst of that city I dug canals, I flooded its site with water, and the very foundations thereof I destroyed. I made its destruction more complete than that by the flood. That in days to come the site of that city, and its temples and gods, might not be remembered, I completely blotted it out with floods of water and made it like a meadow.

DOCUMENT 6

THE BABYLONIAN KING NEBUCHADNEZZAR FORTIFIES BABYLON

An inscription by Nebuchadnezzar II, about 580 B.C.

That no assault should reach the wall of Babylon I did what no earlier king had done. I caused a mighty wall to be built on the east side of Babylon, I dug out a moat and I built a scarp with bitumen and bricks. Its broad gateways I set within it and mounted within them double doors of cedar wood overlaid with copper. In order that the enemy should not press on the flanks of Babylon, I surrounded it with mighty floods, as is the land with the wave-tossed sea.

DOCUMENT 7

BABYLON *HERODOTUS – Describing the city as it was about the time of Nebuchadnezzar II*

Assyria possesses a vast number of great cities, whereof the most renowned and strongest at this time was Babylon, whither after the fall of Nineveh, the seat of government was removed. The following is an exact description of the place. The city stands on a broad plain and is an exact square, fifteen miles in length each way, so that the entire circuit is sixty miles. While such is its size, in magnificence there is no other city that approaches to it. It is surrounded in the first place, by a broad and deep moat, full of water, behind which rises a wall 335 feet wide and 85 feet high.

The city is divided into two portions by the river Euphrates which flows through the middle of it. The city wall is brought down on both sides to the edge of the stream: thence from the corners of the wall there is carried along each bank of the river a fence of burnt bricks. The houses are mostly three and four stories high; the streets all run in straight lines, not only those parallel to the river, but also the cross streets which lead down to the waterside. At the river end of these cross streets are low gates in the fence that skirts the stream, which are, like the great gates in the outer wall, of brass, and open on the water.

The outer wall is the main defence of the city. There is, however, a second inner wall.

DOCUMENT 8

THE CONQUEST OF EGYPT BY THE ASSYRIANS *ESARHADDON – An Assyrian King, 671 B.C.*

From the town of Ishhupri as far as Memphis, the royal residence, a distance of fifteen days' march, I fought daily, without a break, the bloodiest battles against Tirhakah, king of Egypt and Ethiopia, the one accursed of all the great gods. Five times I dealt him incurable wounds with the points of my arrows. I laid siege to Memphis, his royal residence, and conquered it in half a day with mines, breaches and assault-ladders; I destroyed it, I tore down its walls, I burned it with fire. His wife and the women of his palace, his heir and his other children, his possessions, his horses, his cattle in immense quantity I bore away as booty into Assyria. All the Ethiopians did I deport from Egypt, leaving not even one to do homage. Everywhere in Egypt I appointed new kings, governors, officials, maritime overseers, officers and scribes. I instituted sacrifices for Ashur and the other great gods my lords, for all time. I laid upon them the tribute due to me as overlord, to be paid annually without a break.

DOCUMENT 9

ARMY LAWS *HAMMURABI – From his code of laws*

If a soldier who was ordered to go on campaign for the king did not go or hired a substitute, the soldier shall be put to death and the one who was hired shall take over his estate. If a soldier is taken prisoner on active service and his fields are given to another who performs his feudal services for him, then if he returns he shall receive back his fields and resume his feudal services.

If a soldier has sufficient money to ransom himself he shall do so; if not he shall be ransomed from his local temple estate. If there is not enough money in the temple estate then the state shall ransom him because his own fields and house may not be sold to pay his ransom.

If an officer has conscripted a soldier or has accepted a hired substitute then the officer shall be put to death.

If an officer has taken a soldier's property or wronged him or taken the money given to the soldier by the king then the officer shall be put to death.

DOCUMENT 10

DIVORCE, SUMERIAN STYLE *Sumerian marriage contract*

If Enlil-izzu ever says to Ama-sukkal his wife, 'You are no longer my wife', he shall return the nineteen shekels of silver and he shall also weigh out half a mina as her divorce settlement. On the other hand if Ama-sukkal ever says to Enlil-izzu her husband, 'You are no longer my husband', she shall forfeit the nineteen shekels and she shall also weigh out half a mina of silver. In mutual agreement they have sworn this by the king.

DOCUMENT 11

THE POOR IN SUMER *Sumerian proverbs*

1

The poor man is better dead than alive;
If he has bread, he has no salt,
If he has salt, he has no bread,
If he has meat, he has no lamb,
If he has a lamb, he has no meat.

2

You can have a lord, you can have a king,
But the man to fear is the tax collector.

DOCUMENT 12

EDUCATION AT SUMER: A FATHER QUESTIONS HIS SON *From a Sumerian essay written about 2000 B.C.*

Father: Where have you been?
Son: Nowhere.
Father: If you didn't go anywhere why are you lazing about? Go to school, stand in front of the school teacher and recite your homework, open your school bag, write your tablet, and let the monitor write a new tablet for you. When you have finished your work and reported to your monitor, come to me and don't wander about the streets. Be a man. Don't stand about in the public square or wander in the main street. When you are walking in the street don't look all around. Be humble and show fear before your monitor. When you show terror your monitor will like you.

DOCUMENT 13

FARMING IN LOWER EGYPT *HERODOTUS*

At present they obtain the fruits of the field with less trouble than any other people in the world, since they have no need to break up the ground with the plough nor to use the hoe, nor to do any of the work which the rest of mankind find necessary if they are to get a crop; but the husbandman waits till the river has of its own accord spread itself over the fields and withdrawn again to its bed, and then sows his plot of ground, and after sowing turns his swine into it (the swine tread in the seed) after which he has only to await the harvest.

DOCUMENT 14

HARD TIMES IN EGYPT *HEKANAKHTE – A priest writing to his family in about 2000 B.C. and telling them off for complaining*

See, you yourselves are people who eat until you are satisfied. The whole land is dying of starvation, but you are not hungry. I decided our rations for the best. Our rations will be fixed for us according to the state of the inundation.

Be patient all of you. As they say, it is better to be half alive than to die outright. They have started to eat men here; they do not get rations like yours. Be brave therefore until I can come to see you. Give rations to my people according to how they are doing their work. Be very careful because you are eating my rations. Now as for anyone who refuses his rations, let him come here to live with me as I live, but certainly no-one would want to come to me here.

DOCUMENT 15

JUSTICE IN EGYPT *Instructions to the chief minister from the King*

Do not judge inconsistently; the abomination of the divine king is partiality. Look upon him who is known to you in the same way as him who is unknown to you; him who is close to you in the same way as him who is far from you.

Do not send a petitioner away before listening to him. Dismiss him only after telling him why you are dismissing his case, because it is said that a petitioner would rather that you pay attention to what he says than win his case.

Do not be angry with any man without good cause; be angry only when there is good reason to be angry. Inspire fear of yourself so that men are afraid of you because a true magistrate is one of whom people are afraid. But the reputation of a magistrate comes from his giving justice. If people are too frightened of a magistrate then there must be something unjust about him.

DOCUMENT 16

EDUCATION IN EGYPT *Advice to a schoolboy from his father*

I place you at school along with the children of notables to educate you and train you for the work of a scribe. When you get to your work don't be idle. Read diligently from the book and when you do silent arithmetic don't make a noise. Write with your hand and read with your mouth. Ask advice from those who are clever. Spend not a day in idleness or woe betide you, you will be soundly punished. Set not your heart on pleasures or you will be ruined. The ear of a boy is on his back and he pays attention when he is beaten.

I am told that you have stopped writing, that you give yourself up to pleasures. You go from street to street where it smells of beer, to destruction. Beer, it will scare men from you, and it will send your soul to perdition. You have been seen climbing a wall and breaking in. Men run away from you, for you assault them.

However I have seen many like you, that said 'Books are a waste of time'. Yet they became scribes in the end.

DOCUMENT 17

AN EGYPTIAN SCRIBE'S VIEW OF OTHER JOBS

Look for yourself. The washerman spends the whole day going up and down, all his body is weak through whitening the clothes of his neighbours every day and washing their linen. The potter is smeared with earth like a person one of whose folk has died. His hands and feet are full of clay, he is like one who is in the mire. A carpenter carries the timber and stacks it. If he renders today produce of yesterday, woe to his limbs! The shipwright stands behind him to say to him evil things. The outworker who is in the fields has the toughest job of all. He spends the whole day laden with his tools, tied down to his tool-box. But the scribe is the one that reckons the produce of all those. Take note of this.

DOCUMENT 18

DEATH STATEMENT OF THE STEWARD OF THE KEEPER OF THE SEAL *This piece from the Egyptian Book of the Dead contained what the writer hoped to say on Judgement Day, after he had died*

I have not done evil against people. I have not committed wrong in court. I have not known evil and worthless men. I have not done evil things. I have not caused the first work of the day to be done for me. I have not put forward my name for honours. I have not taken any poor man's property. I have not blamed a slave to his master. I have not inflicted pain. I have not made anyone hungry. I have not made anyone weep. I have not committed murder. I have not commanded to murder. I have not caused anyone to suffer. I have not stolen the offerings in the temples . . . I have not given underweight. I have not taken milk from the mouths of children. I have not driven cattle from their pastures. I have not used fish as bait to catch fish. I have not taken water from other men's fields. I am pure! I am pure! I am pure!

DOCUMENT 19

CONFESSION OF A TOMB ROBBER *AMENPNUFER – A twelfth-century stone mason*

I fell into the habit of robbing the tombs in company with the stone-mason Haspwer. Four years ago I joined with the carpenter, Setekhnakhte; the decorator, Rapio; the field labourer, Amenemhab; the carpenter Irenamun; the water pourer, Khaemwese; and with the boatman of the Mayor of Thebes – in all eight men.

We went to rob the tombs in accordance with our regular habit and we found the pyramid of King Sebekamsef, this being not at all like the pyramids and tombs of the nobles which we habitually went to rob.

We broke through the rubble and found this God (king) lying at the back of his burial-place and his queen beside him. We opened their sarcophagi and their coffins in which they were, and found the noble mummy of this King completely bedecked with gold and his coffins were adorned with gold and silver inside and out and inlaid with all kinds of precious stones.

We collected the gold we found on the noble mummy of this god and on the queen and we set fire to their coffins. We took their furniture consisting of articles of gold, silver and bronze, and divided them amongst ourselves.

Thus I, together with other thieves who are with me, have continued to this day in the practice of robbing the tombs and the people of the land who rest in the west of Thebes. And a large number of people of the land rob them as well, and are as good as partners of ours.

DOCUMENT 20

TUTANKHAMEN *HOWARD CARTER – The archeologist who entered the tomb of Tutankhamen (who reigned about 1347-1339 B.C.) in A.D. 1922*

At last we had the whole door clear before us. The decisive moment had arrived. With trembling hands I made a tiny breach in the upper left-hand corner. Darkness and blank space, as far as an iron testing rod could reach. Candle tests were applied as a precaution against possible foul gases, and then widening the hole a little, I inserted the candle and peered in. At first I could see nothing, the hot air escaping from the chamber causing the candle flame to flicker. But presently, as my eyes grew accustomed to the light, details of the room emerged slowly from the mist, strange animals, statues, and gold – everywhere the glint of gold.

DOCUMENT 21

MUMMIES *HERODOTUS – On his travels through Egypt*

First of all with a crooked piece of iron they draw out the brains through the nostrils. Then with a sharp stone they make a cut along the flank and remove all the intestines. Then after filling the belly cavity with pure finely powdered myrrh, cinnamon, and other spices, except frankincense, they sew it up again. After this they put the body in salt, covering it with natron for seventy days; they must not leave it in the salt any longer. When the seventy days are over, they wash the body and wrap it around from head to foot with strips cut from a sheet of fine linen, smeared with gum. Then the relatives take it and have a wooden coffin made shaped like a man, and shutting the body up in it they place it in the sepulchral chamber, setting it upright against the wall.

DOCUMENT 22

THE HYKSOS INVASION *FLAVIUS JOSEPHUS – A Jewish historian of the first century A.D. quoting Manetho, an Egyptian historian of the third century B.C.*

TUTIMAIOS. In his reign, for what cause I know not, a blast of God smote us; and unexpectedly from the regions of the East invaders of obscure race marched in confidence of victory against our land. By main force they seized it without striking a blow; and having overpowered the rulers of the land, they then burned our cities ruthlessly, razed to the ground the temples of the gods, and treated all the natives with a cruel hostility, massacring some and leading into slavery the wives and children of others. Finally they appointed as king one of their number whose name was Salitis; he had his seat in Memphis, levying tribute from Upper and Lower Egypt, and always leaving garrisons behind in the most advantageous places.

DOCUMENT 23

THE DEFEAT OF THE HYKSOS *Inscription of the King Kamose, about 1550 B.C.*

His Majesty spoke to the council of nobles: 'What use to me is my strength! One prince rules in Avaris, another in Ethiopia, and here I am, associated with an Asiatic and a negro. Each has his slice of Egypt, dividing up the land with me. None can rest in peace, despoiled as all are by the taxes of the Asiatics. I will grapple with them and cut open their belly! I will save Egypt and overthrow the Asiatics.

'I went north victoriously to repulse the Asiatics. My valiant army marched before me like a blast of fire. When day broke I pounced on the foe like a falcon; at breakfast time I attacked him. I broke down his walls, I slew his people, I captured his women. My soldiers were as lions with the spoils of the enemy; flocks, hay and honey. They shared out their property with merry heart.'

ACKNOWLEDGMENTS

Illustrations

The British Museum pages 14, 18; The Egyptian Tourist Office pages 15, 16 both pictures; The Mansell Collection pages 3, 6, 8, 10, 20; Paul Popper Ltd pages 4, 12, 13 both pictures, 17, 19.

Documents

D1, 4, 7, 13, *The Persian Wars,* Herodotus, tr. Francis R. B. Godolphin, Random House, Inc; D5, *Land of the Two Rivers,* Leonard Cottrell, Brockhampton Press Limited; D6, 10, *The First Great Civilizations,* Hawkes, Hutchinson Publishing Group Ltd; D16, 18, *The Literature and Mythology of Ancient Egypt,* ed. Joseph Kastner, Allen Lane, 1970, Penguin Books Ltd.